I0491818

Contents

Introduction

I still remember the first time that I have encountered the stock market. Passing by and seeing those mysteriously powerful and yet simple numbers displayed on the school's computer screen, and being explained by the Economics students, who were on a stock-market project at that time, that these numbers were the prices of part of the most renown companies across the country, was absolutely mesmerizing. Till this day, I have known that I would be doing this; I would be owning parts of great companies.

If you are like me, I bet you are also amazed by the easiness and yet majestic power of the stock market. However, you should know that its pretended easiness is as lethal as arsenic. In fact, technologies have given the false appearance that the stock-market investing just some magical clicks which fills your bank account without any effort. But seriously though, why would billionaires work day and night in their stressful positions, if the dollars were just hiding under their computer's mouse? Therefore, a good education is important. Not the classic one (the school system), but the intelligent one.

The Intelligent Investor by Benjamin Graham is, in my and various other successful persons opinions, the Bible of the Investor. This comparison may seem exaggerated, but to be frank I am a bit spiritual with this book. I have seen those following it blindly succeed in their investment career, and I have also seen many, who thought they were smarter than the book, fell into the trap of the devil and lose lots of money. I prefer to stay on the safe side and follow this book because as Warren Buffett famously says, the two rules to succeed in the stock market are Rule.1 NEVER lose money and Rule.2 NEVER forget Rule.1. I do not know for you, but I kind of like these two rules. On this ground, if you are reading this book without having read The Intelligent Investor, I highly recommend that you close it and go buy Graham's book.

If you have read it however, you already know how bulky and how fat of information it is. In fact, I bet it is because of this huge amount of knowledge inscribed in such a big book, that lead certain investor to forget certain rules and laws, which if not obeyed, led almost certainly to losses. Because of the high number of pages in it, I have taken a copybook and a pen right at the start and I have written all the important points that I have found important. In so doing, I have arrived at my summary which I am presenting to you and which I, of course, cherish.

This summary is a tool which will let you re-read The Intelligent Investor without going through hundreds of pages again. Time is scarce and we cannot dedicate it to re-read a bulky book even once. And due to this, this summary comes as a blessing. Sometimes when the gains are high and your strategy seems flawless, you lose contact with the reality and start thinking that you are invincible. Keeping an eye on the rules of Graham let you remember how cautious you should be and how doubtful you must be, in order to know exactly where you are going. Value Investing is based on the long-term, and on the long run, too much is forgotten. For me I try to read it every month and I would recommend it to you also.

You cannot know how happy I am that a reader, you, will use this summary as his investing tool, as his pocket Bible, in order to succeed in his financial life. If you could earn only one penny by having a rapid glance at a rule in this book, my heart will be overflowed with joy. And for this dear reader, I say a big thank you for choosing this book.

Without losing more of your time, I wish you a great success as you dive again into Benjamin Graham's genius.

Gregory from Wake & Walk.

How to use this book

This summary is fully written from the book The Intelligent Investor. I have put the most important rules and lessons from the book and classified the various information under certain symbols. These symbols will let you know where the definitions, the knowledge, the things to avoid and any other things are. Here are the keys:

DEFINITION: All the definitions across this book are written in capital letters and so are easily recognizable.

- This square-like symbol is dedicated solely for all the quotes inside the book. As you may know, there are many interesting and really motivating quotes throughout The Intelligent Investor and I have judged it important to include the in this summary.

➢ I think this is the most popular symbol across the summary. This is to represent all the things that you should be careful about and many of which you should fear! In fact, much of Graham's book tell you what NOT to do in the stock market. Therefore, I urge you to take all the words after this symbol very seriously across the summary.

- ✓ This symbol is way less popular. These are just positive points about the market that your attention should go to.
- ❖ This symbol represents the important knowledge that you should have before entering the market. These are not definitions but are the knowledges on the way to do things concretely.
- ○ This symbol is for the Anecdotes. These are metaphoric situations described by Graham and how they relate to some situations in the stock market.

Throughout the book you will also meet some equations written by me. I am fond of mathematics and it helps me better understand some concepts. Even if this is not the case for everyone, I have decided to include it anyway and if they could help you, it would be great. If not, they are described also in words by Graham, so you do not have to worry.

With these symbols, your re-reading of the essentials of The Intelligent Investor should be way smoother. I recommend reading it on one go the first time and then let it lie near your bed for every time that you want to have a glimpse at the rules written by Benjamin Graham.

With this, I wish you a good reading and a nice adventure.

Wake & Walk

summarizes
The
Intelligent
Investor

- "Those who do not remember the past are condemned to repeat it."

SPECULATORS: Buy because a stock or market has gone up and sell because it has declined.

INVESTORS: Buy because a stock or market has declined and sell because it has gone up.

- ✓ The underlying principles of sound investment shall not alter from decade to decade, but the application of these principles must be adapted to significant changes in the financial mechanisms and climate.

- ➤ Enthusiasm in the Stock Market almost invariably lead to disaster.

DEFENSIVE/PASSIVE INVESTOR: Places his chief emphasis on the avoidance of serious mistakes or losses. His second aim will be freedom from effort, annoyance, and the need for making frequent decisions.

ACTIVE/AGGRESSIVE/ENTERPRISING INVESTOR: Devote time and care to the selection of securities that are both sound and more attractive than average

➢ Never succumb to the 'certainty' that any industry will outperform all others in the future (E.g. at Pg. 6)

❖ What it means to be an "intelligent" investor?
1. Not related to IQ or grade scores.
2. Patience, Discipline and Eager to learn.
3. Harness our emotion and think for ourselves.

▪ "This kind of intelligence is a trait more of the character than of the brain."
✓ It relates to emotional intelligence

! Books to Read:

1. When Genius Failed, Roger Lowenstein.
2. The South Sea Bubble, John Carswell.

➢
I. Obvious prospects for physical growth in a business do not translate into obvious profits for investors.
II. The experts do not have dependable ways of selecting and concentrating on the most promising companies in the most promising industries.

➤ The intelligent investor realizes that stocks become more risky, not less, as their price rise – and less risky, not more, as their prices fall.

✓ The intelligent investor dreads a bull market, since it makes stocks more costly to buy. And conversely, should welcome a bear market since it puts stocks back on sale.

INVESTMENT OPERATION: An investment operation is one which, upon thorough analysis, promises safety of principal and an adequate return. Operations not meeting these requirements are speculative.

! Book to Read: Security Analysis

❖ Signs of Unintelligent Speculation:
1. Speculating when you think you are investing.
2. Speculating seriously instead of as a pastime when you lack proper knowledge and skill for it.
3. Risking more money in speculation than you can afford to lose.

➤ Every non-professional who operates on margin should recognize that he is ipso facto speculating.

MARGIN: Enables you to buy stocks using money you borrow from the brokerage firm.

> ➤ Everyone who buys a so-called 'hot' common-stock, or makes a purchase in any way similar thereto, is either speculating or gambling.

In case of trial in speculation, read Pg. 22 first paragraph

- ❖ Results to be expected by Defensive Investor (Around 1965):
1. Divide holdings between high-grade bonds and leading common stocks.
2. 25%<proportion in bonds<75%, 25%<proportion in common stocks<75%
3. Simplest choice: 50-50 proportion
4. If felt that market is dangerously high, reduce common-stock component to 25%
5. If felt that a decline in stock prices was making them increasingly attractive, advance common-stock component to 75%

INVESTMENT GRADE: An investment grade is a rating that indicates that a municipal or corporate bond has a relatively low risk of default. Bond rating firms, such as Standard&Poor's and Moody's, use different designations consisting of upper and lower-case letters 'A' and 'B' to identify a bond's credit-quality rating, 'AAA' and 'AA'(high credit quality) and 'A' and 'BBB'(medium credit-quality) are considered investment grade. Credit ratings below these designations ('BB', 'B', 'CCC', etc....) are considered low credit quality, and are referred as 'junk bonds'.

➢ The Future of Security Prices is NEVER predictable.

RATE OF RETURN: A rate of return is the gain or loss on an investment over a specified time-period, expressed as a percentage of the investment's cost. Gains on investments are defined as income received plus any capital gains realized on the sale of the investment.

❖ 3 practices of the defensive investor:
1. Purchase of shares of well-established investment funds as an alternative to creating his own common-stock portfolio.
2. Dollar-cost averaging: meaning that the practitioner invests in common-stocks the same number of dollars each month or each quarter.
3. Vary his holdings of common stocks between 25% and 75%, in inverse relationship to the action of the market.

❖ Results to be expected by the Aggressive Investor:

To enjoy a reasonable chance of continued better than average results, the investor must follow policies which are

1) Inherently sound and promising.
2) Not popular on the market.

✓ A common stock may be undervalued because of lack of interest or unjustified popular prejudice.

▪ "Buying neglected and therefore undervalued issue for profit generally proves a protracted and patience-trying experience. And selling short a too popular and therefore overvalued issue is apt to be a test not only of one's courage and stamina but also of depth of one's pocketbook. The principal is sound, its successful application is not impossible, but it is distinctly not an easy art to master."

! Book To Read: The House of the Rothschild: Money's Prophet , by Niall Ferguson.

▪ "All human unhappiness comes from one single thing: not knowing how to remain at rest in a room." – Blaise Pascal.

- ❖ Investing consists of 3-elements:
1. You must thoroughly analyze a company, and the soundness of its underlying businesses before you buy its stock.
2. You must deliberately protect yourself against serious losses.
3. You must aspire to adequate, not extraordinary performance.

- ➢ Wall Street (like any other market), like Vegas or the racetrack, has calibrated the odds so that the house always prevails in the end, against everyone who tries to beat the house at its own speculative game.

- ➢ People who invest makes money for themselves; people who speculate makes money for their brokers.

- ➢ Confusing speculation with investment, Graham warns, is always a mistake. (See E.g. Pg. 36)

- ➢ The intelligent investor has no interest in being temporarily right. To reach your long-term financial goals, you must be sustainably and reliably right.

➢ The intelligent investor never dumps a stock purely because its share price has fallen; he ALWAYS as first whether the value of the company's underlying businesses has changed.

I. You must NEVER delude yourself into thinking that you are investing when you are speculating.
II. Speculating becomes MORTALLY DANGEROUS the moment you begin to take it seriously.
III. You must put strict limits on the amount you are willing to wager.

- "For better or worse, the gambling instinct is a part of human nature. So, it is futile for most people even to try suppressing it. But you must confine and restrain it."

- "Americans are getting stronger. Twenty years ago, it took two people to carry ten dollars' worth of groceries. Today, a five-year old can do it." – Henry Youngman.

❖ THE MONEY ILLUSION:

If you receive a 2% raise in a year when inflation runs at 4%, you will almost certainly feel better than you will if you take a 2% pay out during a year when inflation is zero. Yet both changes in your salary leave you in a virtually identical position, -2% worse off after inflation.

➢ So long as the nominal (or absolute) change is positive, we view it as a good thing – even if the real (or after inflation) result is negative.

! Article To Read: Money Illusion by Eldar Shafir,Peter Diamond and Amos Tversky.

➢ It is clear that those with a fixed dollar income will suffer when the cost of living advances, and the same applies to a fixed amount of dollar principal. Holders of stocks, on the other hand, have the possibility that a loss of the dollar's purchasing power may be offset by advances in their dividends and the prices of their shares.

▪ "You've got to be careful if you don't know where you're going, cause you might not get there." -Yogi Berra

➢ The intelligent investor MUST NEVER forecast the future exclusively by extrapolating the past.

- "The higher they go, the harder they fall."

❖ Simple, skeptical questions as an enduring antidote to bull-market baloney:

1) Why should the future returns of stocks always be the same as their past returns?
2) When every investor comes to believe that stocks are guaranteed to make money in the long run, won't the market end up being wildly overpriced?
3) And once that happens, how can future returns possibly be high?

✓ The value of an investment is, an always should be, a function of the price you pay for it.

➢ Since the profits that companies can earn are finite, the price that investors should be willing to pay for stocks must also be finite.

➢ Focusing on the market's recent returns when they have been rosy will lead to a quite illogical and dangerous conclusion that equally marvelous results could be expected for common stocks in the future.

❖ The stock market's performance depends on 3 factors:

1. Real growth (the rise of companies' earnings and dividends)
2. Inflationary growth (the general rise of prices throughout the economy)
3. Speculative growth/or decline (any increase or decrease in the investing public's appetite for stocks)

■ "Blessed is he who expecteth nothing, for he shall enjoy everything."

FALSE CLAIM! The rate of return which the investor should aim for is more or less proportionate to the degree of risk he is ready to run.

The rate of return sought should be dependent on the amount of intelligent effort the investor is willing and able to bring to bear on his task.

I. The minimum return goes to our passive investor, who wants both safety and freedom from concern.
II. The maximum return goes to the alert and enterprising investor who exercises maximum intelligence and skill.

- ❖ Possible Action for the Defensive Investor:
- • Keep the ratio of stocks to bonds at 50:50.
- • Raise percentage in common stocks during bear market.
- • Reduce percentage in stocks when prices are abnormally high.

DANGER: With human nature, it is difficult to assure the behavior of the investor during the circumstances.

- ❖ Good Behavior of the Defensive Investor:
- • Maintain the ratio of stocks to bonds at 50:50
- • When stocks grow, sell and use to compensate for bonds and maintain at 50:50

- ▪ "When you leave it to chance, then all of a sudden you don't have any more luck" – Basketball coach Pat Riley

- ▪ "The enterprising approach is physically and intellectually taxing, while the defensive approach is emotionally demanding" – Charles Elis

- • If you have time to spare. Are highly competitive, think like a sports fan, and relish complicated intellectual challenge, then the active approach is up your alley.

- If you always feel rushed, crave simplicity, and do not relish thinking about money, then the passive approach is for you.

! Article to Read: Miswanting by Daniel Gilbert & Timothy Wilson

➤ There is no correlation between your age and the amount of your portfolio in stocks

❖ Fundamental circumstances of life determining risk:
1. Are you single or married? What does your spouse do for a living?
2. Do you or will you have children? When will tuition bills hit home?
3. Will you inherit money, or will you end up financially responsible for aging, ailing parents?
4. What factors might hurt your career? (If you work for a bank or a homebuilder, a jump in interest rates could put you out of a job. If you work for a chemical manufacturer, soaring oil prices could be bad news.)
5. If you are self-employed, how long do businesses similar to yours tend to survive?
6. Do you need your investments to supplement your cash income?

7. Given your salary and your spending needs, how much money can you afford to lose on your investments?

- If, considering these factors, you feel you can take the higher risks inherent in greater ownership of stocks, you belong around Graham's minimum of 25% in bonds or cash.
- If not, then steer mostly clear of stocks, edging toward Graham's maximum of 75% in bonds or cash.
- Change the target percentages only as life circumstances change
  Do not buy more stocks because the stock market has gone up; do not sell because it has gone down.

➤ Rebalance on a predictable, patient schedule- not so often that you will drive yourself crazy and not so seldom that your targets will get out of whack.

Suggestion: Rebalance every six months

❖ Why not 100% stocks?

Graham advises you never to have more than 75% of your total assets in stocks. But is putting all our money into the stock market inadvisable for everyone? For a tiny minority of investors, a 100% stock portfolio may make sense. You are one of them if you:

1. Have set aside enough cash to support your family for at best one year
2. Will be investing steadily for at least 20years to come
3. Survived the bear market that began in 2000(applicable for bear markets onward)
4. Did not sell stocks during the bear market that began in 2000(applicable for bear markets onward)
5. Bought more stocks during the bear market that began in 2000(applicable for bear markets onward)
6. Have read chapter 8 of The Intelligent Investor and implemented a formal plan to control your own investing behavior.

Unless you can honestly pass all these tests, you have no business putting all your money in stocks. Anyone who panicked in the last bear market is going to panic in the next one – and will regret having no cushion of cash and bonds.

❖ Rules for the Common-Stock component (Defensive Investor):
1. There should be adequate, though not excessive, diversification. This might mean a minimum of ten different issues and a maximum of about thirty.
2. Each company should be large, prominent, and conservatively financed. Indefinite as these adjectives must be, their general sense is clear.
3. Each company should have long record of continuous dividend payments. Today's defensive investor should probably insist on at least 10 years of continuous dividend payments. Even insisting on

20years of uninterrupted dividend payments would not be overly restrictive.

4. The investor should impose some limit on the price he will pay for an issue in relation to its average earnings over, say, the past seven years.

Suggestion: Let limit be set at 25 times such average earnings and not more than 20 times those of the last 12-month period. Such restriction would eliminate nearly all the strongest and most popular companies from the portfolio. In particular it would ban virtually the entire category of growth stocks.

EARNINGS: It typically refer to after-tax net income.

GROWTH STOCK: The term "growth stock" is applied to one which has increased its per-share earnings in the past at well above the rate for common stocks generally and is expected to continue to do so in the future.

❖ The "Rule of 72":

To estimate the length of time an amount of money takes to double, simply divide its assumed growth rate into 72. At 6%, for instance, money will double in 12 years (72/6=12). At 7.1%, a growth stock will double its earnings in just over 10 years (72/7.1=10.1years)

PRICE EARNINGS RATIO: The "price/earnings ratio" of a stock or of a market average like the S&P 500 – stock index is a simple tool for taking the market's temperature. If, for example, a company earned $1 per share of net income over the past year and its stock is selling at $8.93 per share, its price/earnings ratio would be 8.93; if however the stock is selling at $69.70, the price/earnings ratio would be 69.7. In general, a price/earnings ratio below 10 is considered low, between 10 and 20 is considered moderate and greater than 20 is considered expensive.

➢ Earnings multiplier (P/E ratio) measures how much investors are willing to pay for a stock compared to the profitability of the underlying business.

▪ The young man, who saves $1000 a year and expects to do better gradually, finds himself with though for still different reasons ……. The balance is so modest that it seems hardly worthwhile for him to undergo a tough educational and temperamental discipline in order to qualify as an aggressive investor. Thus, a simple resort to our standard program for the defensive investor would be at once the easiest and the most logical policy.

▪ Let us ignore human nature at this point……. There is a great advantage for the young capitalist to begin his financial education and experiences early. If he is going to operate as an aggressive investor, he is certain to make some mistakes and to take some losses. Youth can stand for disappointment and stand by them. We urge the beginner in security-buying not to waste his efforts and his money in trying to beat the market.

- "Human felicity is produced not so much by great Pieces of good Fortune that seldom happen, as by little Advantages that occur every day." – Benjamin Franklin

- How defensive you should be, depends less on your tolerance for risk than on your willingness to put time and energy into your portfolio.

- "After you burn your mouth on hot milk, you blow on your yoghurt." – Turkish Proverb

- The decision of whether to own stocks today has nothing to do with how much money you might have lost by owning them a few years ago.

- The defensive investor must always defend against the belief that you can pick stock without doing any homework.

❖ Lynch's Rule: "You can outperform the experts if you use your edge by investing in companies or industries you already understand"
Lynch's rule can work only if you follow its corollary as well: "Finding the promising company is only the first step. The next step is doing the research."

! Book to Read: One Up on Wall Street, Peter Lynch with John Rothschild.

▪ Becoming more familiar with a subject does not significantly reduce people's tendency to exaggerate how much they actually know about it. – documented by Psychologists led by Baruch Fischhoff.

o Anecdote:

On the TV news, isn't it always the neighbor or the best friend or the parent of the criminal who says in a shocked voice, "He was such a nice guy"? That's because whenever we are too close to someone or something, we take our beliefs for granted, instead of questioning them as we do when we confront something more remote.

➢ The more familiar a stock is, the more likely it is to turn a defensive investor into a lazy one who thinks there's no need to do any homework. DON'T LET THAT HAPPEN TO YOU.

! Paper to Read:

"Do Those Who Know More Also Know More about How Much They Know?", Sarah Lichstein & Baruch Fischhoff; Organizational Behaviour and Human Performance vol.20 no2 Dec 1977 pg. 159-183

> ➢ If you find yourself trading more than twice a year – or spending more than an hour or two per month, total, on your investments- then something has gone badly wrong. Do not let the ease and up-to-the-minute feel of the internet seduce you into becoming a speculator. A defensive investor runs and wins the race by sitting still.

> ❖ As the financial markets heave and crash their way up and down day after day, the defensive investor can take control of the chaos. Your very refusal to be active, your renunciation of any pretended ability to predict the future, can become your most powerful weapons. By putting every investment decision on autopilot, you drop any self-delusion that you know where stocks are headed, and you take away the market's power to upset you no matter how bizarrely it bounces.

- ➤ All investors should be wary of new issues- which means, simply, that these should be subjected to careful examination and unusually severe tests before they are purchased.

- ➤ Most new issues are sold under "favorable market conditions" – which means favorable for the seller and consequently less favorable for the buyer.

- ❖ Recently, finance professors Owen Lamont of the University of Chicago and Paul Schultz of the University of Notre Dame have shown that corporation choose to offer new shares to the public when the stock market is near a peak.

! Paper to Read:

Lamont's "Evaluating Value Weighting Corporate Events & Market Timing"

Schultz's "Pseudo Market Timing and the Long-Run Performance of IPOs"

http://papers.ssrn.com

- ✓ An elementary requirement for the intelligent investor is an ability to resist the blandishments of salesmen offering new common-stock issues during bull markets.

- "The punches you miss are the ones that wear you out" – Boxing Trainer Angelo Dundee

- ➢ For the aggressive as well as the defensive investor what you don't do is as important to your success as what you do.

- o Anecdote:

Buying a bond only for its yield is like getting married only for the sex. If the thing that attracted you in the first place dries up, you'll find yourself asking, "What else is there?" When the answer is "Nothing", spouses and bondholders alike end up with broken hearts.

- ➢ Day Trading is one of the best weapons ever invented for committing financial suicide.

- ➢ Someone who can't hold on to stocks for more than a few months at a time is doomed to end up not as a victor but as a victim.

- ➢ The psychologists Daniel Kahneman and Amos Tversky have shown when human estimate the likelihood or frequency of an event, we make that judgement based not on how often the event has actually occurred, but on how vivid the past examples are.

➢ Buying IPOs is a bad idea because it flagrantly violates one of Graham's most fundamental rules: No matter how many other people want to buy a stock, you should buy only if the stock is a cheap way to own a desirable business.

❖ Weighing the evidence objectively, the intelligent investor should conclude that IPO does not stand only for "initial public offering". More accurately, it is also shorthand for:

- It's Probably Overpriced
- Imaginary Profits Only
- Insiders Private Opportunity or
- Idiotic, Prosperous and Outrageous

✓ The enterprising investor, by definition, will devote a fair amount of his attention and efforts toward obtaining a better than run-of-the-mill investment result.

❖ The activities especially characteristic of the enterprising investor in the common-stock field may be classified under 4 hoards

1. Buying in low markets and selling in high markets
2. Buying carefully chosen "growth stocks"
3. Buying bargain issues of various types
4. Buying into "special situations"

GROWTH STOCK: Stock of components that will do better than average over a period of years.

❖ Two catches to this simple idea:
A. Common stocks with good records and apparently good prospects sell at correspondingly high prices. The investor may be right in his judgement of their prospects and still not fare particularly well, merely because he has paid in full (and perhaps overpaid) for the expected prosperity.
B. The judgement as to the future may prove wrong. Unusually rapid growth cannot help up forever; when a company has already registered a brilliant expansion, its very increase in size makes a repetition of its achievement more difficult.

ENTERPRISING INVESTOR: An enterprising investor is not one who takes more risk than average or who buys "aggressive growth" stocks; an enterprising investor is simply one who is willing to put in extra time & effort in research.

❖ Calculate Price/Earnings ratio based on a multiyear average of past earnings. That way, you lower the odds that you will overestimate a company's value based on a temporarily high burst of profitability. Imagine that a company earned $3 per share over the past 12months, but an average of only 50cents per share over the previous 6 years.

At 25 times the $3 it earned in the most recent year; the stock would be priced at $75 (Price=P/E × E)

But at 25 times the average earnings of the past seven years ($6 in total earnings divided by 7 equals 85.7cents per share in average annual earnings), the stock would be priced at only $21.43.

Which number you pick makes a big difference.

❖ Fundamental law of Stock Market:

If we assume that it is the habit of the market to overvalue common stocks which have been showing excellent growth or are glamorous for some other reason, it is logical to expect that it will undervalue – relatively at least- companies that are out of favor because of unsatisfactory developments of temporary nature.

OVERVALUATION $\propto$ EXCELLENT GROWTH or GLAMOUR

UNDERVALUATION $\propto$ TEMPORARY UNSATISFACTORY DEVELOPMENT

➢ Enterprising Investor must concentrate on the larger companies that are going through a period of unpopularity.

➢ While small companies may also be undervalued for similar reasons and in many cases may later increase their earnings and share price, they entail the risk of a definitive loss of profitability and also of protracted neglect by the market in spite of better earnings.

❖ Large companies have a double advantage over the others. First, they have the resources in capital and brain power to carry them through adversity and back to satisfactory earnings base. Second, the market is likely to respond with reasonable speed to any improvement shown.

BARGAIN ISSUE: We define a bargain issue as one which, on the basis of facts established by analysis, appears to be worth considerably more than it is selling. Let us suggest that an issue is not a true "bargain" unless the indicated value is at least 50% more than the price.

❖ Two tests by which a bargain common stock is detected.
1. By the method of appraisal

Relies largely on estimating future earnings and then multiplying these by a factor appropriate to the particular issue.

2. The value of the business to a private owner
   This value also is often determined chiefly by expected future earnings. But in the 2nd test more attention is likely to be paid to the realizable value of the assets, with particular emphasis on the net current assets or working capital.

➤ The market is fond of making mountains out of molehills and exaggerating ordinary vicissitudes into major setbacks.

❖ Two major sources of undervaluation:
1. Currently disappointing results.
2. Protracted neglect or unpopularity
   NEITHER can be relied on as a guide (alone) to successful common-stock investment.
✓ The type of bargain issue that can be most readily identified is a common stock that sells for less than the company's net working capital alone, after deducting all prior obligations.

NET WORKING CAPITAL: Company's current assets (such as cash, marketable securities, and inventories) minus its total liabilities (including preferred stock & long-term debt).

SECONDARY COMPANIES: We have defined a secondary company as one that is not a leader in a fairly important industry.

Exception: Growth Stock is not ordinarily considered "secondary".

- ❖ If most secondary issues tend normally to be undervalued, what reason has the investor to believe that he can profit from such a situation?
  1. Dividend return is relatively high.
  2. The reinvested earnings are substantial in relation to the price paid and will ultimately affect the price.
  3. A bull market is ordinarily most generous to lower-priced issues
  4. Even during relatively featureless market periods a continuous process of price adjustment goes on, under which secondary issues that were undervalued may rise at least to the normal level.
  5. The specific factors that in many cases made for a disappointing record of earnings may be corrected by advert of new conditions.

- ➢ Investment policy depends in the first place on a choice by the investor of either the defensive or the aggressive role.

❖ Aggressive investor must have a considerable knowledge of security values – enough, in fact, to warrant viewing his security operations as equivalent to a business enterprise.

➢ There is no room in this philosophy for a middle ground or a series of gradations, between the passive and the aggressive status.

➢ As an investor you cannot soundly become "half a businessman", expecting thereby to achieve half the normal rate of business profits on your funds.

▪ "It requires a great deal of boldness and a great deal of caution to make a great fortune; and when you have got it, it requires ten times as much wit to keep it." – Nathan Mayer Rothschild.

▪ "Life can only be understood backwards – but it must be lived forwards." – Danish Philosopher Søren Kierkegaard

➢ In the financial markets, hindsight is forever 20/20 but foresight is legally blind.

➢ A great company is not a great investment if you pay too much for the stock.

o Anecdote:

Fundamental law of Financial Physics: The bigger they get, the slower they grow.

$$\frac{d}{dt}(size\ of\ company) \propto \frac{1}{size\ of\ company}$$

➢ The intelligent investor gets interested in big growth stocks not when they are at their most popular but when something goes wrong.

Foreign Policy Read Pg. 187

✓ Since common stocks, even of investment grade, are subject to recurrent and wide fluctuations in their prices, the intelligent investor should be interested in the possibilities of profiting from these pendulum swings.

❖ Two possible ways:
1. Timing!! (SPECULATOR)
2. Pricing.

TIMING: Endeavour to anticipate the action of the stock market. Buy or hold when the future course is deemed to be upward, to sell or refrain from buying when the course is downward.

PRICING: Endeavour to buy stocks when they are quoted below their fair value and to sell them when they rise above such value.

Less ambitious form of pricing is the simplest effort to make sure that when you buy you do not pay too much for your stocks. Suitable for Defensive Investor.

"Shrewd Investor": One who bought in a bear market when everyone else was selling and sold out in a bull market when everyone else was buying.

- ❖ Bull Markets Characteristics (U.S.A):
1. Historically high price level
2. High Price/ Earnings ratios
3. Low dividend yields as against bond yields
4. Much speculation on margin
5. Many offerings of new common-stock issues of poor quality.

- ➢ Any approach to moneymaking in the stock market which can be easily described and followed by a lot of people is by its terms too simple and too easy to last.

❖ Reason for the fading of the Easy Ways to Make Money in the Stock Market:
1. Natural tendency of trends to reverse over time or "regress to the mean".
2. Rapid adoption of the stock-picking scheme by large numbers of people, who pile in and spoil all the fun of those who got there first.

➢ Every investor who own common stocks must expect to see them fluctuate in value over the years.

▪ "All things excellent are as difficult as they are rare." – Spinoza.

➢ A serious investor is not likely to believe that the day-to-day or even month-to-month fluctuations of the stock market make him richer or poorer.

❖ Business Valuations versus Stock Market Valuations:
1) On the one hand, his position is analogous to that of a minority shareholder or silent partner in a private business.
   His results are entirely dependent on the profits of the enterprise or on a change in the underlying value of its assets.
2) On the other hand, the common-stock investor holds a piece of paper, an engraved stock certificate, which

can be sold in a matter of minutes at a price which varies from moment to moment – when the market open, that is – and often is far removed from the balance sheet value.

Net asset value/ Book Value/ Balance-Sheet Value/Tangible-Asset Value/ Net Worth/ Total Value of a company's physical and financial assets minus all its liabilities.

$$Book\ Value = \frac{Total\ Shareholder's\ Equity - Soft\ Assets}{Number\ of\ Shares\ Outstanding}$$

SOFT ASSETS: Things such as goodwill, trademarks and other intangibles.

> ➤ A stock does not become a sound investment merely because it can be bought at close to its asset value (book value per share).

> ❖ Additional Info needed:
1. A satisfactory ratio of earnings to price.
2. A sufficiently strong financial position.
3. The prospects that its earnings will at least be maintained over the years.

But note this important fact: The true investor scarcely ever is forced to sell his shares, and at all other times he is free to disregard the current price quotation. He needs to pay attention to it and act upon it only to the extent that it suits his book, and no more (only to the extent that the price is favorable enough to justify selling the stock). Thus, the investor who permits himself to be stampeded or unduly worried by unjustified market declines in his holdings is perversely transforming his basic advantage into a basic disadvantage. That man would be better off if his stocks had no market quotation at all, for he would then be spared then mental anguish caused to him by other persons mistakes of judgement.

❖ Three different factors for price fluctuations of convertible bonds and preferred stocks:
1. Variations in the price of the related common stock.
2. Variation in the credit standing of the company.
3. Variations in the general interest ratios.

o Anecdote:

Would you willingly allow a certifiable lunatic to come by at least five times a week to tell you that you should feel exactly the way he feels? Would you ever agree to be euphoric just because he is – or miserable just because he thinks you should be? Of course not. You'd insist on your right to take control of your own emotional life, based on your experiences and your beliefs. But when it comes to their financial lives, millions of people let Mr. Market tell them how to feel and what to do – despite the obvious fact that, from time to time, he can get mistier than a fruitcake.

✓ The intelligent investor shouldn't ignore Mr. Market entirely. Instead, you should do business with him – but only to the extent that it serves your interests. Mr. Market's job is to decide whether it is to your advantage to act on them. You do not have to trade with him just because he constantly begs you to.

! To Read: "Thoughts on Security Analysis" , Benjamin Graham, Financial History Magazine no 42 March 1991 p8.

➢ Investing intelligently is about controlling the controllable.

❖ What can't be controlled?
Whether the stocks or funds you buy will outperform the market today, next week, this month or this year.

❖ What can be controlled?
• Your Brokerage costs
  By trading rarely, patiently and cheaply.
• Your ownership costs

By refusing to buy mutual funds with excessive annual expenses.

- Your Risk
  By deciding how much of your total assets to put at hazard in the stock market, by diversifying and by rebalancing.
- Your Tax Bills (U.S.A)
  By holding stocks for at least one year and, whenever possible, for at least five years, to lower your capital-gains liability.
- Your Own Behavior

➢ Investing isn't about beating others at their game. It's about controlling yourself at your own game.

➢ Psychologists have shown that if you present people with a random sequence and tell them that it's unpredictable, they will nevertheless insist on trying to guess what's coming next.

➢ Our brains are designed to perceive trends even where they might not exist. After an event occurs just two or three times in a row, regions of the human brain called anterior cingulate and nucleus accumbens automatically anticipate that it will happen again.

If it does repeat, a natural chemical called dopamine is released, flooding your brain with soft euphoria.

Thus, if a stock goes up a few times in a row, you reflexively expect it to keep going – and your brain chemistry changes as the stock rises, giving you a "natural high". You affectively become addicted to your own predictions.

But when a tock drops, that financial loss fires up your amygdalate - the part of the brain that processes fear and anxiety and generates the famous "fight or flight" response that is common to all cornered animals. You can't help feeling fearful when stock prices are plunging.

> Brilliant Psychologists Daniel Kakermann and Amos Tversky have shown that the pain of financial loss is more than twice as intense as the pleasure of an equivalent gain.

! To Read: "Are You Wired for Wealth?" Money, October 2002 Pg. 74-83 Jason Zweig.

❖ If after checking the value of your stock portfolio at 1:24 PM, you feel compelled to check it all over again at 1:37 PM, ask yourself these questions:
● Did I call a real estate agent to check the market price of my house at 1:24 PM? Did I call back at 1:37 PM?
● If I had, would the price have changed? If it did, would I have rushed and sell my house?
● By not checking, or even knowing the market price of my house from minute to minute, do I prevent its value from rising over time?

- The schoolteacher asks Billy Bob: "If you have twelve sheep and one jumps over the fence, how many sheep do you have left?
  Billy Bob answers. "None."
  "Well," says the teacher, "you sure don't know your subtraction."
  "Maybe not," Billy Bob replies, "but I damn sure know my sheep."
  -As told by Prof. Henry T.C. Hu of the University of Texas School of law.

➤ Most investors simply buy a fund that has been going up fast, on the assumption that it will keep going.
  .....
  Unfortunately, in the financial markets, luck is more important than skill.

❖ Points on which financial scholars are unanimous:
1. The average fund does not pick stocks well enough to overcome its costs of researching and trading them.
2. The higher a fund's expenses, the lower its returns.
3. The more frequently a fund trades its stocks, the less it tends to earn.
4. Highly volatile funds which bounce up and down more than average are likely to stay volatile.
5. Funds with high past returns are unlikely to remain winners for long.

❖ Qualities of funds who beat the index:
1. Their managers are the biggest shareholders.
2. They are cheap.
3. They dare to be different.
4. They shut the door.
5. They don't advertise.

❖ When to sell?
1. A sharp and unexpected change in strategy.
2. An increase in expenses.
3. Large & frequent tax bills.
4. Suddenly erratic returns.

▪ "If you're not prepared to stay married, you shouldn't get married."

➢ Businessmen seek professional advice on various elements of their business, but they do not expect to be told how to make profit.

❖ Sources of advice on investments:
• A relative or a friend, presumably knowledgeable in securities.
• A local (commercial) banker.
• A brokerage firm or investment banking house.

- A financial service or periodical.
- An investment counselor.

> If the investor is to rely chiefly on the advice of others in handling his funds, then either he must limit himself and his advisers strictly to standard, conservative and even unimaginative forms of investment, or he must have an unusually intimate and favorable knowledge of the person who is going to direct his funds into other channels.
> If ordinary business or professional relationship exists between the investor and his advisers, he can be receptive to less conventional suggestions only to the extent that he himself has grown in knowledge and experience and has therefore become competent to past independent judgement on the recommendations of others.

! Book To Read: The Go-Go Years, John Brook.

- "I feel grateful to the Milesian wench who, seeing the philosopher Thales continually spending his time and contemplation of the heavenly vault and always keeping his eyes raised upward, put something in his way to make him stumble, to warn him that it would be time to amuse his thoughts with things in the clouds when he had seen to those at his feet. Indeed, she gave him or her good counsel, to look rather to himself than to the sky." – Michel de Montaigne.

❖ Signals showing that you need advice:
1. Big losses.
2. Busted budgets.
3. Chaotic portfolios (not diversified)
4. Major changes.

➤ Before you place your financial future in the hands of an adviser, it's imperative that you find someone who not only makes you comfortable but whose honesty is beyond reproach."

▪ "Trust, then verify." – Ronald Reagan.

❖ The security analyst deals with the past, the present and the future of any given security issue.
● He describes the business.
● He sets forth its strong & weak points.
● Its possibilities & risks.
● He estimates its future earning power under various assumptions or as a "best guess"
● He makes elaborate comparisons of various companies or of the same company at various times.
● He expresses an opinion as to the safety of the issue, if it is a bond or a preferred stock or as to its attractiveness as a purchase, if it is a common stock.

❖ Common-Stock Analysis:

- The ideal form of common-stock analysis leads to a valuation of the issue which can be compared with the current price to determine whether or not the security is an attractive purchase.

- This valuation would ordinarily be found by estimating the average earnings over a period of years in the future and then multiplying that estimate by an appropriate "capitalization factor".

- The now-standard procedure for estimating future earning power starts with average past data for physical volume, prices received and operating margin.

- Future sales (in currency) are then projected on the basis of assumptions as to the amount of change in volume and price level over the previous base.

- These estimates are grounded first on general economic forecasts of gross national product, and then on special calculations applicable to the industry and company in question.

❖ Other factors than average future earnings:

1. General Long-Term Prospects.
   No one really knows anything about what will happen in the distant future, but analysts and investors have strong views on the subject just the same. These views are reflected in the substantial differentials between the price/earnings ratios of individual companies and of industry groups.

2. Management.

3. Financial Strength & Capital Structure
   Stock of a company with a lot of surplus cash and nothing ahead of the common is clearly a better purchase (at the same price) than another one with the same per share earnings but large bank loans and senior securities.
4. Dividend Record
   One of the most persuasive tests of high quality is uninterrupted record of dividend payments going back over many years.
5. Current Dividend rate.

❖ Foreshortened formula for the valuation of growth stocks:

Value=Current(Normal)Earnings×(8.5+2×Expected Annual Growth Rate)

❖ Two Part Appraisal Process:
   a) First work out the "past performance value", which is based solely on the past record.
   b) Consider to what extent the value based solely on past performance should be modified because of new conditions expected in the future.

▪ "Would you tell me, please, which way I ought to go from here?"
   "That depends a good deal on where you want to get to," said the cat
   -Lewis Caroll, Alice's Adventures in Wonderland.

➢ Gather evidence from financial statements to help answer two overriding questions:

❖ What makes this company grow? Where do (and where will) its profits come from?

❖ Problems to watch for:

1) The company is a "serial acquirer"
An average of more than two or three acquisitions a year is a sign of potential trouble.

2) The company is an OPM addict, borrowing debt or selling stock to raise boatloads of Other People's Money.
These fat infusions of OPM are labeled "cash from financing activities" on the statement of cashflows in the annual report.
If cash from operating activities is consistently negative while cash from financing activities is consistently positive, the company has a habit of craving more cash than its own businesses can produce and you shouldn't join the enablers of that habitual abuse.

3) The company is a Johnny-One-Note
It relies on one customer (or a handful) for most of its revenues.

➢ Among the good signs:

1) The company has a wide 'moat' or competitive advantage.
Several forces can widen a company's moat:

I.   A strong brand identity.

II.   A monopoly or near monopoly of the market.

III.   Economies of scale.

IV.   A resistance to substitution.

! Book To Read: Competitive Strategy, Michael E.Parker

2) The company is a marathoner, not a sprinter.

3) The company sows and reap

No matter how good its products or how helpful its brands, a company must spend some money to develop new businesses.

➢ The quality & conduct of management

• A company's executives should say what they will do, then do what they said.

• Managers should forthrightly admit their failures and take responsibility for them, rather than blaming all-purpose scapegoats like "the economy", "uncertainty", or "weak demand".

➢ Questions to help determine whether the people who run the company will act in the interests of the people who own the company:

1) Are they looking out for No. 1?

Obscenely obese payday suggests that the firm is run by the managers, for the managers.

- If a company reprices (or reissues or exchanges) its stock options for insiders, stay away/
- A manager can't legitimately be your partner if he keeps selling while you're buying.

2) Are they managers or promoters?
   - Executives should spend most of their time managing their company in private, not promoting it to the investing public.
   - Are the company's accounting practices designed to make its financial results transparent or opaque?
     If
     I. "nonrecurring" charges keep recurring.
     II. "extraordinary" items crop up so often that they seem ordinary.
     III. Acronyms like EBITDA take priority over net income.
     IV. "pro forma" earnings are used to cloak actual losses.

     You may be looking at a firm which do not put its shareholders' long-term interests first.

> Financial Strength & Capital Structure:

A good business is one which generates more cash than it consumes.

OWNER EARNING=Net Income + Amortization&Depreciation - Normal Capital Expenditures

To fine-tune the definition of owner earnings also subtract from the reported net income:

- Any costs of granting stock options.
- Any "unusual", "nonrecurring" or "extraordinary" changes.
- Any "income" from the company's pension fund.

➢ Advice to the investor that cannot avoid being contradictory in his inspirations:
1. Don't take a single year's earnings seriously.
2. If you do pay attention to short-term earnings, look out for booby traps in the per-share figures.

➢ The more seriously investors take the per-share earnings figures as published, the more necessary it is for them to be on their guard against accounting factors of one kind and another that may impair the true comparability of the numbers.

❖ Accounting factors to be on guard:
a) Special Charges.
b) Reduction in the normal income tax deduction by reason of past losses.

c) Dilution factor implicit in the existence of substantial amounts of convertible securities or warrants.

d) "Pro forma" or "as if" financial statements which report a company's earnings as if Generally Accepted Accounting Principles (GAAP) did not apply.

e) Dilutive effect of issuing millions of stock options from reducing the value of the common stock.

f) Unrealistic assumptions of return on the company's pension funds.

g) "Special Purpose Entities" or affiliated firms or partnership that buy risky assets or liabilities of the company and thus "remove" these financial risks from the company's balance sheet.

h) Treatment of marketing or other "soft" costs as assets of the company rather than as normal expenses of doing business.

- "You can get ripped off easier by a dude with a pen than you can by a dude with a gun." -Bo Diddley

PRO FORMA EARNINGS: Pro-forma earnings enable companies to show how well they might have done if they hadn't done as badly as they did

➢ As an intelligent investor, the only thing you should do with pro-forma earnings is ignore them.

- ❖ Pointers to help avoid buying stock that turns out to be as an accounting bomb:
1. Read backwards
   When you research a company's financial reports, start reading on the last page and slowly work your way towards the front.
   Anything that the company doesn't want you to find is buried in the back.
2. Read the notes
   Never buy a stock without reading the footnotes to the financial statements.

- ❖ One keynote describes
- How the company recognizes revenue.
- Records inventories.
- Treats installment or contract sales.
- Expenses its marketing costs.
- Accounts for the other major aspects of its business.

- ❖ Another footnote to watch for disclosures about
- Debt.
- Stock options.
- Loans to customers.
- Reserves against losses.
- Other 'risk factors' that can take a big champ out of earnings.

- ❖ Beware of technical terms like

- 'Capitalized', 'deferred' and 'restructuring' and plain English words signaling that the company has altered its accounting practices like 'began', 'change' and 'however'.

3. Read more.
   Learn about financial reporting.

! Books to Read:

I.   Financial Statement Analysis, Martin Fridson & Fernando Alvarez.
II. The Financial Numbers Game, Charles Mulford & Eugene Comiskey
III. Financial Shenanigans, Howard Schilit.

❖ Figures to look for, for a good summary of a stock:
A. Capitalization
- Price of Common Stock
- Number of shares of common stock
- Market Value of Common Stock
- Bonds & Preferred Stock
- Total Capitalization
B. Income Items
    - Sales (Actual)
    - Net Income (Actual)
    - Earnings Per Share (Actual)
    - Earnings Per Share Averages (3-year gap)

- Current Dividend
C. Balance Sheet Items (Actual)
- Current Assets
- Current Liabilities
- Net Assets for Common Stock
- Book Value per share

❖ Key ratios relating performance & price of a stock to look for

Ratio:

- Price/Earnings (Actual)
- Price/Earnings (Average)
- Price/Book Value
- Net/Sales
- Net per Share/Book Value
- Dividend Yield
- Current Assets/Current Liabilities
- Working Capital/Debt
- Earnings growth per Share
  Average vs average

Price Record:

Beginning to 2 years before Actual

- Low
- High

Actual

- Low
- High

Major Points to Note

Having read The Summary of The Intelligent Investor, you should now know these points:

- **A stock is PART OF A COMPANY and not only a mysterious ticker-symbol.**
  If you would buy a company, you would try to make the best guess of the price of it to avoid overpaying, isn't it? Then why would one not do it for part of a company? You should consider your stock as a company, with the price of the latter being determined by the demand in buying your company.
- **You should buy what you know.**
  Again, if you are buying a company, would you buy one that you do not even know what it does? You should absolutely know how your company makes money and you should judge based on its business model whether it is viable long term or not. A company solves a problem; it satisfies a demand. If a company does not meet a demand, or does it poorly, then why are you doing business? Therefore, when you buy a stock, you should see if ever the company has a good business model or not.
- **Buy assets, not debt.**
  If the company you are planning to buy is flooded of debt, then you will pay for headaches. That is not what you want, hopefully. Therefore, you should seek companies which are low on debt and high on assets. Moreover, the companies you search for should have

a good CURRENT RATIO (Current Assets divided by Current Liabilities) to ensure that your company will survive any crisis and unpredicted change in external conditions.

- **Seek for traps in the company's accounting.**
  The traps in the accounting are often dissimulated in the Statement of Profit and Loss. You should dedicate your research not only to balance sheets and income statements but also to Cash Flow Statements. Cash Flow Statements are way harder to falsify as it models the exact cash inflow and outflow of the company for a period. Therefore, dedicate much education to the understanding of the Cash Flow. Some books are recommended in the summary for this purpose.

- **BUY LOW and SELL HIGH.**
  After determining that the company you are watching is a great one, now comes the time of the deal. If the company is worth, let us say, 1 million and the seller is giving it to you for 750k, would you not have a large smile on your face knowing that you have saved 250k? That is the same deal for stocks. Seek for low prices, buy in bear markets. And when the price jumps over your valuation in a bull market or else, sell it and cash in. The work of the Investor is to evaluate and to bargain.

- **YOU and ONLY YOU are the master of your decisions.**
  Base your decisions on facts and YOUR OWN interpretation. Do not let others influence your mind. And by that, day-to-day prices are defined as others

trying to influence you. Do not day trade. Base your decisions to buy and sell solely on your opinion alone. No one cares more for your money than yourself, so be your own expert.

With these lessons, I wish you and I know that your success in the stock market is inevitable. Turn on your computer, start your research, and make your money into money.

"Money makes money. And the money that makes money makes more money." -Benjamin Franklin

ABOUT WAKE & WALK

"Take the money in your wallet and invest it in your mind. And in return, your mind will fill up your wallet."
-Benjamin Franklin

My name is Gregory, I am from a third-world country and one of my goals in life is to be financially independent. This means that I do not want to think anymore of money problems; if I need or want something, I should be able to afford it and not wait for the end-of-month check.

To do this I have tried of course to do a business, but this is not as easy as it may seem. I have tried many things online and I have failed many times. After that I have tried hard and have not seen something worth out of it, I have been despaired. But then, by trying to not give up, an idea has come to my mind, my passion is to learn.

I had realized this till my young age, but I have never known how this could be monetized. This is not really what we could call "talent". So, I have tried other things, but I was never good at them. A few weeks ago, I was reflecting on what I could do, and my summary came to my mind. Would someone not need such a summary as me? This is where the idea of Wake & Walk came to my mind.

This name, Wake & Walk, was originally chosen for another thing. I have bought this site's domain and I have tried to make it in affiliate marketing, but I have soon realized that this was not viable. And since I already had the domain, I have taken it up for my new idea: a publishing company.

This is not a publishing company yet, but it will be, I am sure. My goal is to make Wake & Walk's books the best. As you can guess, my start will be in doing summaries. The book categories will of course be about finance, sales, personal development and anything which will contribute to the success of the readers. I love to learn, and I love summarizing, and above all it is a pleasure for me to help and to change people's lives. And therefore, I will monetize this passion. Later, with more money, I would be publishing books of others and doing their summaries at the same time, and through my brand, these great authors' books will sell with little marketing.

This may seem as a big dream, too big to realize, but if you are reading this dear reader, then there is no doubt that it will come true! And for this, I want to express all my gratitude to you. You are the one to make a little boy's dream possible, and I hope to help you more in the future with my summaries.

Dear reader, know that I heartily wish your success and I hope to further broaden our relation in the future. Until then, make your money into money.

Sincerely,

Gregory from Wake & Walk.